Pebble® Plus

Australian Animals

Koalas

Sara Louise Kras

raintree
a Capstone company — publishers for children

Raintree is an imprint of Capstone Global Library Limited, a company incorporated in England and Wales having its registered office at 264 Banbury Road, Oxford, OX2 7DY – Registered company number: 6695582

www.raintree.co.uk
myorders@raintree.co.uk

Edited by Jessica Server
Designed by Charmaine Whitman
Picture research by Jo Miller
Production by Katy LaVigne
Originated by Capstone Global Library Ltd
Printed and bound in India

ISBN 978 1 4747 7552 6 (hardback)
22 21 20 19 18
10 9 8 7 6 5 4 3 2 1

ISBN 978 1 4747 6044 7 (paperback)
23 22 21 20 19
10 9 8 7 6 5 4 3 2 1

British Library Cataloguing in Publication Data
A full catalogue record for this book is available from the British Library.

Acknowledgements
We would like to thank the following for permission to reproduce photographs:
Alamy: Bill Bachman, 19, Juergen Hasenkopf, 20; Dreamstime: Michael Elliott, 13; Minden Pictures: Suzi Eszterhas, 15; Shutterstock: Holli, 17, HTurner, 9, 21, krithnarong Raknagn, 11, Maeery, 7, mark higgins, cover, Nick Fox, 5, worldwildlifwwonders, 1
Design elements: Shutterstock: Pyty (map), oksanka007.

Every effort has been made to contact copyright holders of material reproduced in this book. Any omissions will be rectified in subsequent printings if notice is given to the publisher.

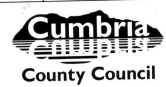

Contents

Living in Australia

What is that grey, furry animal in the tree? It is a koala. Koalas are mammals. Many people think they are a type of bear, but they are not.

Koalas live in Australia.

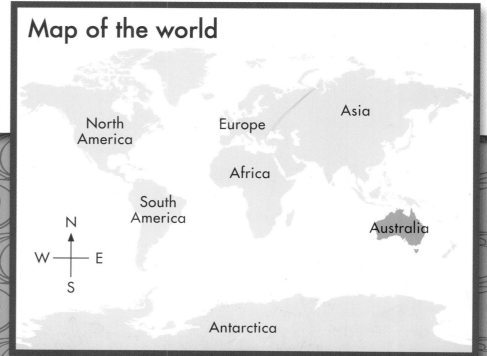

Map of the world

North America

Europe

Asia

Africa

South America

Australia

N
W E
S

Antarctica

Koalas do not live in any other country. They spend most of their lives in eucalyptus trees.

Koalas live in eastern Australia.

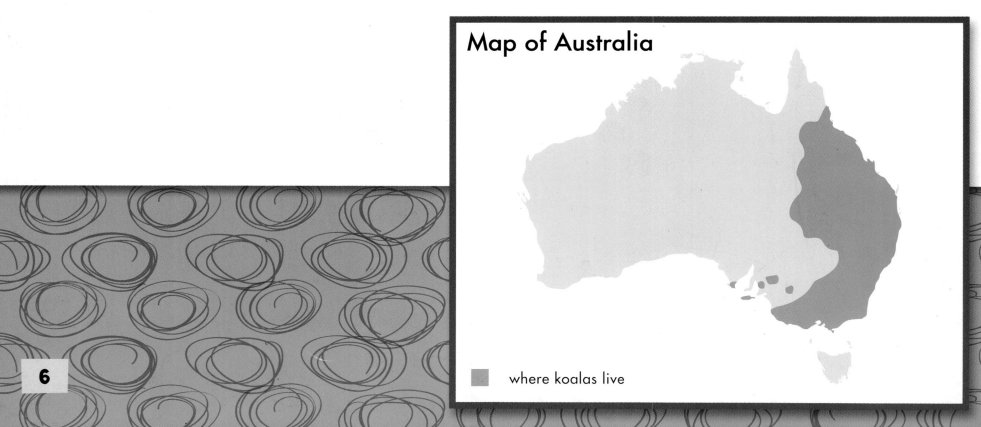

Map of Australia

where koalas live

Koalas have strong arms and legs, which help the koalas to climb in trees. They have two thumbs and sharp claws on each hand to hold on to branches.

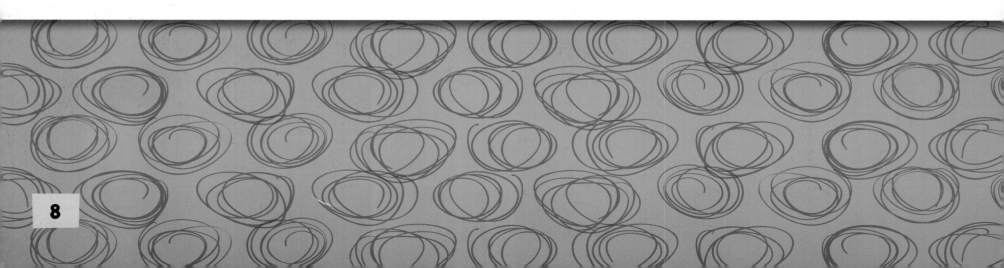

claws

Eating and drinking

Koalas munch on eucalyptus leaves. They have a good sense of smell. They use their noses to find the best leaves to eat.

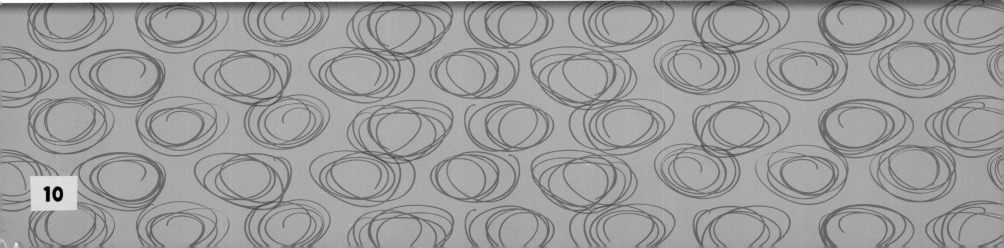

Koalas do not need to leave the trees to get a drink. They get water from eating lots of juicy leaves.

Growing joeys

Koalas belong to a group of animals called marsupials. Marsupials have pouches on their bellies. Newborn koalas are called joeys. They are about the size of a jellybean.

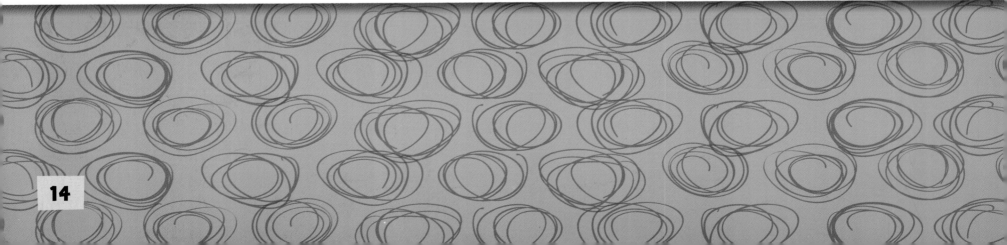

Joeys live in their mothers' pouches until they are about one year old. The mothers teach their joeys how to climb and find food. Then the young koalas can live on their own.

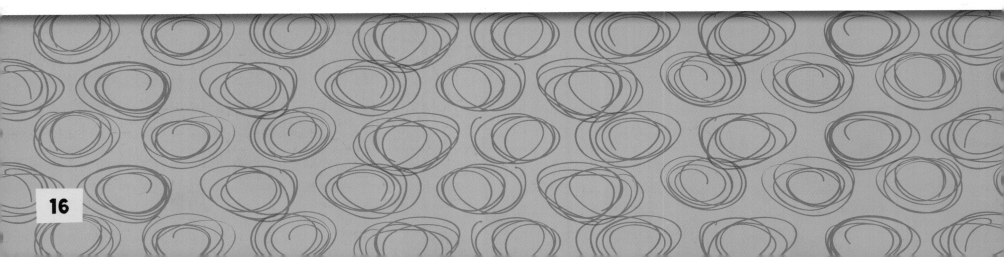

Staying safe

People are the biggest danger to koalas. People cut down eucalyptus trees to use the land and the wood. Cars can hit and kill koalas too.

Some lands have been set
aside for koalas to live in.
These land are called reserves.
The koalas that live there are
protected and safe from harm.

Glossary

eucalyptus tall evergreen tree with a strong scent; koalas eat eucalyptus leaves

joey young koala

marsupial animal that carries its young in a pouch

pouch pocket-like flap of skin

protected kept safe from danger

reserve land that is protected so that animals may live there safely

Find out more

Baby Animals in Pouches (Baby Animals and Their Homes), Martha E. H. Rustad (Raintree, 2017).

Koalas (National Geographic Kids Readers), Laura Marsh (National Geographic Kids, 2014)

The Australian Animal Atlas, Leonard Cronin & Marion Westmacott (Allen & Unwin, 2018)

Websites

This National Geographic web page has lots of fun facts about koalas:
www.natgeokids.com/uk/discover/animals/general-animals/ten-facts-about-koalas/

Learn more facts about koalas at this website:
www.sciencekids.co.nz/sciencefacts/animals/koala.html

This website has fun facts, videos and pictures of koalas:
www.activewild.com/koala-facts-for-kids/

Comprehension questions

1. Where in the world are koalas found?

2. In what kind of tree do koalas live?

3. How long does a joey stay in its mother's pouch?

Index